Contents

Useful stuff

COPY THE TEXTURES YOU SEE on everyday objects to make your drawings look like real machines. Use the equipment shown below to get different effects.

paintbrush

charcoal

4B soft pencil

HB pencil

felt tips

oil pastels

Colour in a drawing with water-soluble coloured pencils. Use a wet paintbrush to soften the colour and make it look more like paint.

water-soluble coloured pencils

coloured pencils

rubber

pencil sharpener

Get drawing in your sketchbook... try out all the machines in this book...

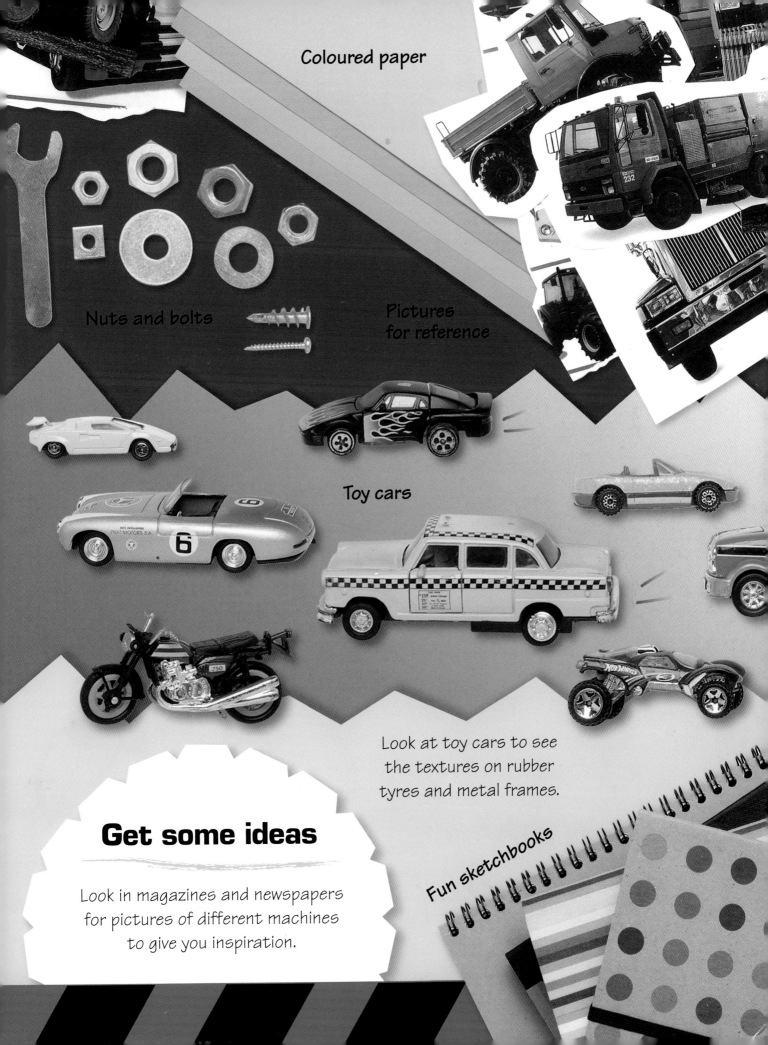

Coloured paper

Nuts and bolts

Pictures for reference

Toy cars

Look at toy cars to see the textures on rubber tyres and metal frames.

Get some ideas

Look in magazines and newspapers for pictures of different machines to give you inspiration.

Fun sketchbooks

Zip!

High-speed,
jet-engine
aeroplane

Photo gallery

MACHINES COME IN A HUGE variety of shapes and sizes. As well as working through the projects in this book, try using the images below for inspiration. That way you can turn out a steam train, a ferry boat, a bicycle, and lots, lots more!

Steam train

1868

Bicycle

Cleeeeeeear the road!

Drag car

I can draw

nines

LONDON, NEW YORK, MUNICH,
MELBOURNE, and DELHI

Designed by Karen Hood, Penny Lamprell
& Sonia Moore
Illustrated by the Peter Bull Art Studio
Written and edited by Carrie Love
& Lorrie Mack
Photography by Andy Crawford

Publishing managers Susan Leonard
& Joanne Connor
Production Seyhan Esen-Yagmurlu
DTP designer Almudena Díaz
Consultant Emma Drew

First published in Great Britain in 2006
by Dorling Kindersley Limited
80 Strand, London WC2R ORL

A Penguin Company

2 4 6 8 10 9 7 5 3 1

ISBN-13 978-1-4053-1507-4
ISBN-10 1-4053-1507-5

Colour reproduction by ICON, United Kingdom
Printed and bound in Slovakia
by Tlaciarne BB S.R.O.

Discover more at
www.dk.com

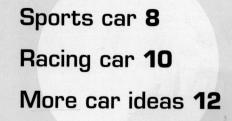

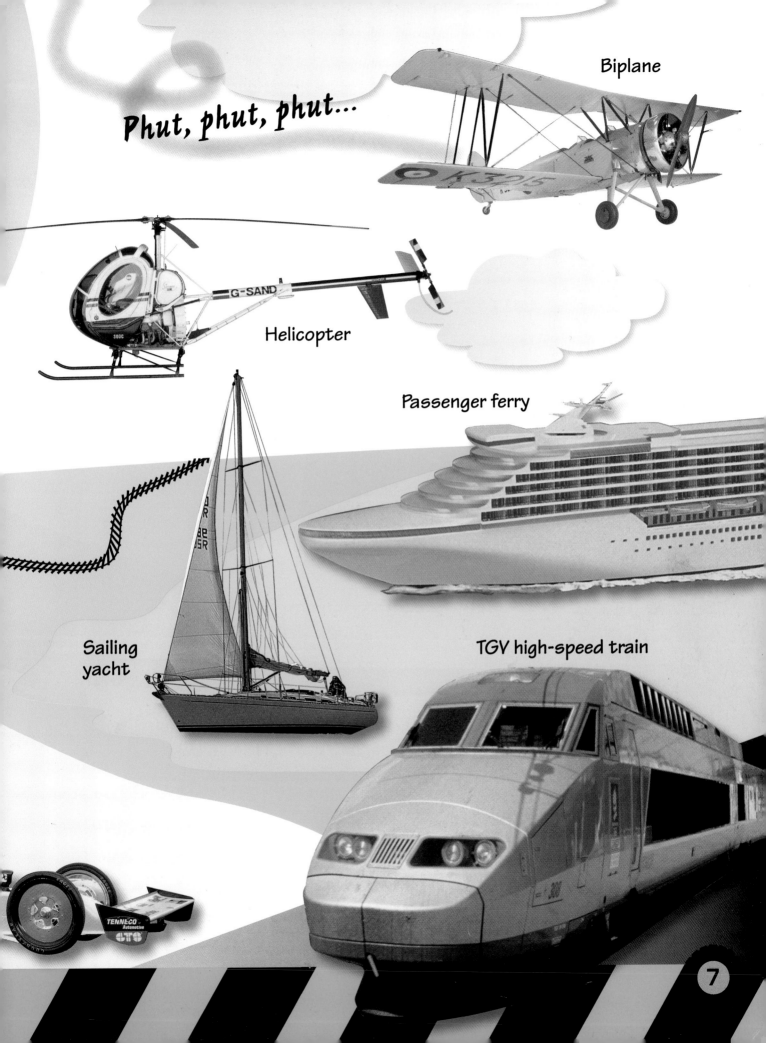

Phut, phut, phut...

Biplane

Helicopter

Passenger ferry

Sailing yacht

TGV high-speed train

1 Make a straight line for your sports car to sit on, then draw two circles the same size for its front and back tyres. Following the drawing below, outline the car's shape.

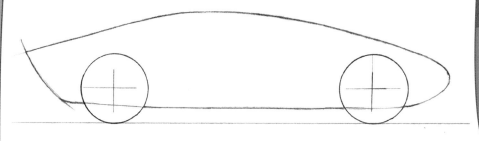

2 Changing your outline slightly, fill in the shapes of the front of the car, the windows, and the wheel arches.

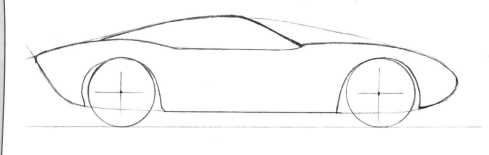

3 Fill in details such as the door and its handle, the window bars, the seats, and the headlamps. Outline the hub caps on the tyres. Don't forget to rub out the circles and lines from step 1.

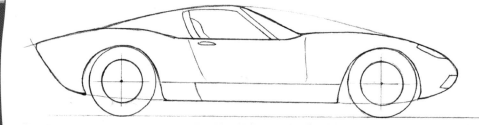

Sports car

Designed mainly to reach high speeds and look good, most sports cars are built to travel on ordinary roads (not race tracks). Some are quite small, some have very low seats, and many are uncomfortable to ride in, but their owners love them anyway.

Finish off by finding a picture of sporty hub caps that you can copy, to make sure the ones on your sports car are detailed and realistic.

Vrroom!

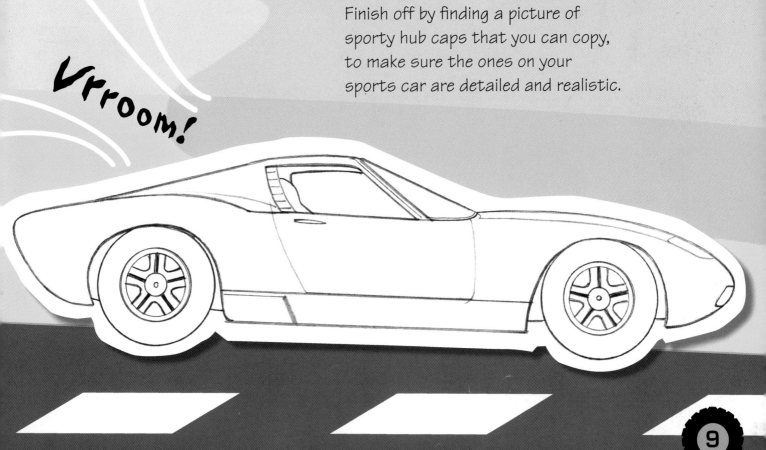

1 Start by drawing a straight line for the road or track your racing car will sit on. Now draw a circle at each end, making the one on the right a little smaller. These will be the front and back tyres.

2 Join the front of the car to the back tyre with a curved line. This will give the front a pointed shape so it cuts through the wind when it's racing. Draw another line above the road to finish off the outline.

Nee-oowww

3 Sketch in the shape of the cockpit (where the driver sits), then use your rubber to take away the part of the long, curved line above it. Add the safety bar and body details.

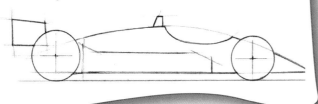

4 Fill in the wing mirror, the windscreen, and the back "wing", which works in the opposite way to aeroplane wings – it holds the car down to the ground instead of lifting it up.

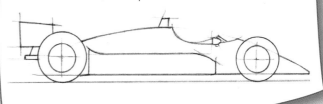

Finish off by adding the air intakes and hub caps. Remember that the front and back wheels are different!

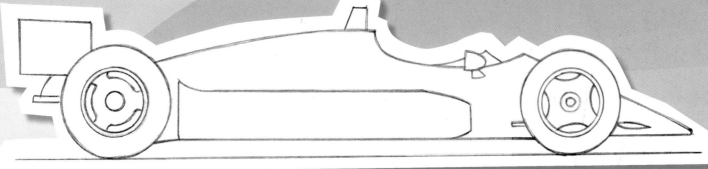

Racing car

Some cars are built specially to race around a track rather than to take people from place to place. Because their only purpose is to go very fast, they don't look like ordinary cars.

WHEN YOU'VE DRAWN all the cars in this book, look through books and magazines to find inspiration for your automobile art. In the meantime, here are some more cool wheels to be getting on with.

More car ideas

Saab Sonet

Rally-racing car

Ford sedan

Alfa Romeo

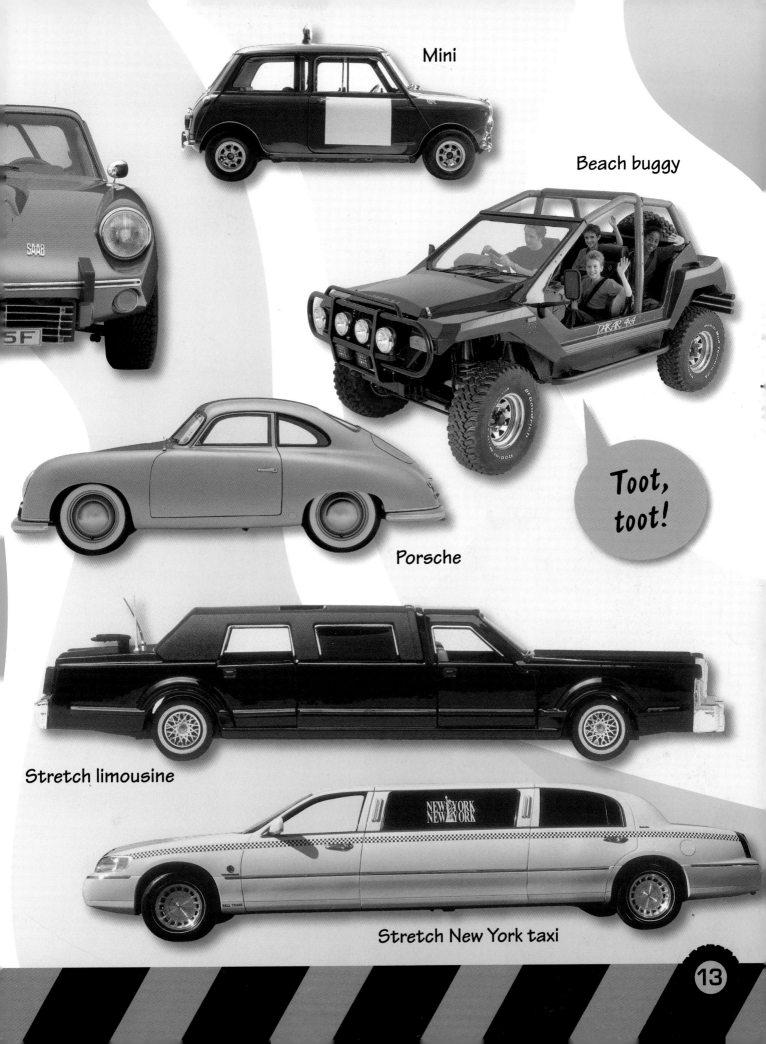

Mini

Beach buggy

Porsche

Toot, toot!

Stretch limousine

Stretch New York taxi

1 Using mostly straight lines, draw shapes for the wings, the tail, and the main body of the plane in the middle of your page.

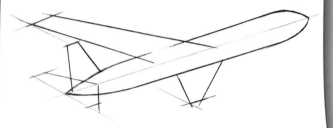

2 Give the aeroplane engines using four small, squashed ovals. The plane can't fly without its engines!

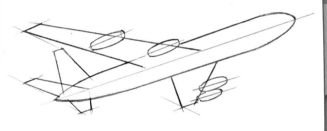

3 Draw the cockpit windows as well as adding some more details to the wings and engines.

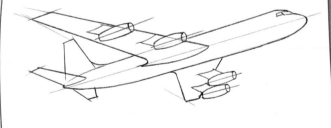

4 Keep adding details until you have a finished aeroplane. You could draw a few clouds at the very top of your page for your plane to fly through!

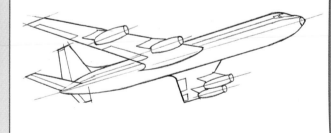

Aeroplane

Up, UP, UP, AND AWAY! Watch the aeroplane take off from the runway and fly up into the clouds.

Add more details like windows and doors. Use shading on the insides of the engines.

Stealth bomber

DESIGNED SO THAT ENEMIES HAVE TROUBLE DETECTING IT, the stealth bomber is an expensive US military aircraft. It has a wingspan of 52 metres (172 feet) and its engines are inside the plane to muffle the noise they create.

1 Start off with three basic lines drawn at the angles shown below.

2 Add to these three lines to create your stealth bomber's fuselage (main body), wings, and rudders.

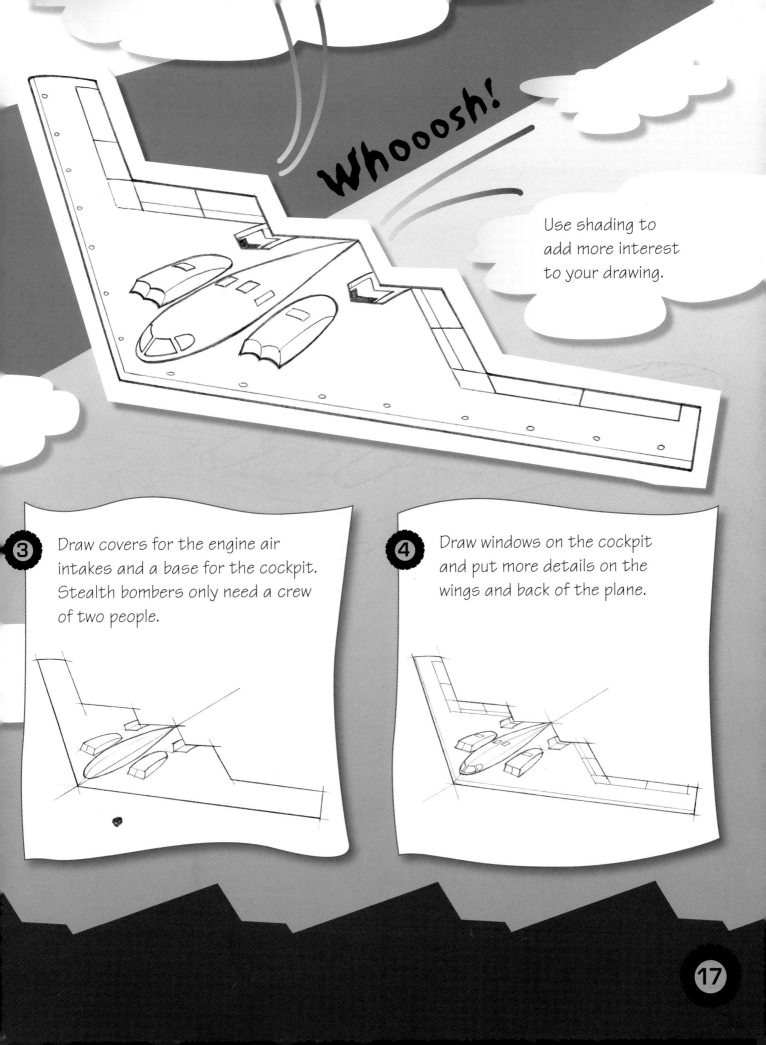

Whooosh!

Use shading to add more interest to your drawing.

3 Draw covers for the engine air intakes and a base for the cockpit. Stealth bombers only need a crew of two people.

4 Draw windows on the cockpit and put more details on the wings and back of the plane.

Each commercial aeroplane is painted in special colours to show which company – or country – owns it. This design is called its 'livery'.

soft pastel, for soft shading

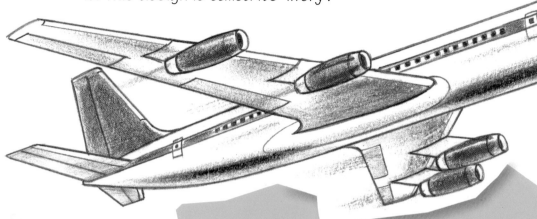

oil pastels

Hide or highlight?

THREE OF THESE MACHINES are painted in bright colours so people will see and recognize them quickly. The fourth machine needs to be almost invisible to do its job. Can you guess which one this is?

Flashy sports cars often have hubcabs that match their shiny paintwork.

felt tips

coloured
pencils

This stealth
bomber is night-
sky blue all over.

Racing-car colours let
everybody know who is
sponsoring the team.

11

felt tips

Shading

A DD INTEREST AND DEPTH to your drawings using shading. Try out the different materials below to create a range of shades in black and grey as well as experimenting with other colours.

pastel, for soft shading

felt-tip pen, for strong flat colour

HB pencil, for general outline and solid shading

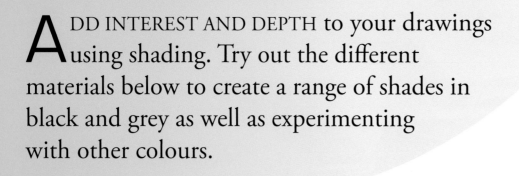

oil pastel, for heavy colour

crayon, for soft shading

rubber for smudging

2B, 3B, and 4B soft pencils, for shading

Types of shading

Create a range of effects with different shading methods.

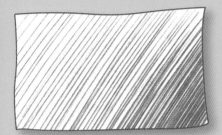

Soft, diagonal lines will add depth to your drawing, but make sure not to press too hard.

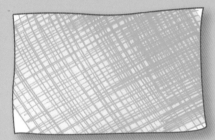

When cross hatching, draw lines in two directions, one over the other, pressing lightly.

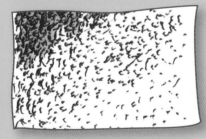

For stippling, create shading by using lots of tiny dots.

Look at these drawings of planes. Shading has made the one below more interesting.

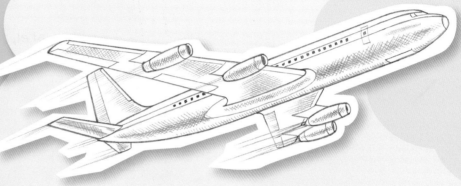

Make your plane more exciting and lifelike with exhaust smoke coming out of the engines.

Compare these images (right) to see how shading can make your drawing better.

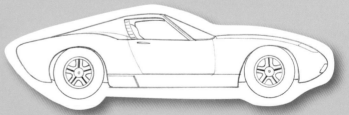

Use smudged lines at the back of the car to make it look as if it's moving.

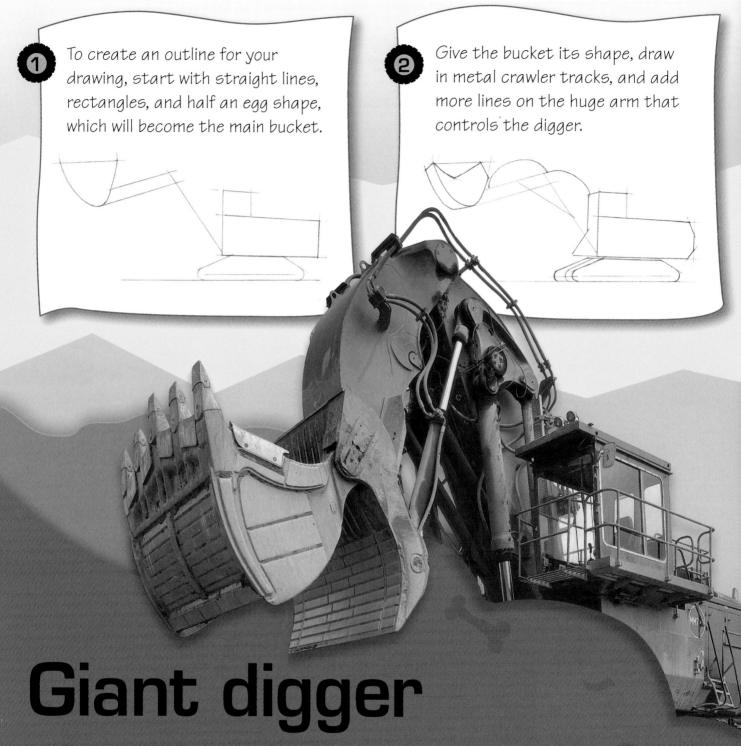

① To create an outline for your drawing, start with straight lines, rectangles, and half an egg shape, which will become the main bucket.

② Give the bucket its shape, draw in metal crawler tracks, and add more lines on the huge arm that controls the digger.

Giant digger

THESE MONSTER MACHINES are used in mines and quarries. Their teeth can cut away at solid rock, and move thousands of tonnes of earth or stone every day. One of these diggers weighs about 24 times as much as a really big truck.

3 Keep adding detail to the bucket, the arm, the bottom of the digger, and the tracks, then sketch in the windows of the driver's cab.

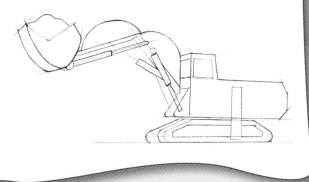

4 Fill in the cab roof, the high access ladder, and the main body of the machine, where the engine lives.

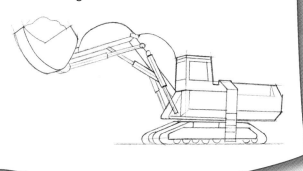

Use fine lines and shading to fill the bucket with rocks, and make the tubes, nuts, tracks, and ground surface look realistic.

CRRRunch

1 The framework of a roller is made up of lots of simple lines and shapes like a plastic toy. Use circles, cylinders, squares, and rectangles to start you off.

2 Even the basic details take the form of straight lines and simple curves. Create the bars around the wheels, for example, with parallel lines and half circles.

3 Draw the cab windows and window bars, and the body markings. Try using a bit of shading to make some details – such as tyres and bars – look 3D.

Roller

USED IN LAYING hard surfaces, rollers have three huge wheels, which are actually drums filled with water. They press down on the tar-and-stone surface of a new road to make it smooth and flat.

Chugga, chugga

Finish off with more shading, and extra detail on the drum wheels and the body.

1 Begin by outlining the dumper's body, the lifting machine underneath, and its two huge wheels — each one of them is taller than a horse!

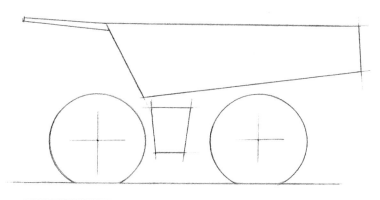

2 Now add the cab, where the driver sits, give more shape to the truck, and draw some lines to show the shape of the dumper body.

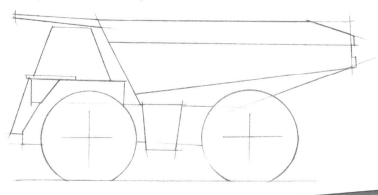

3 The driver's cab door and windows come next, as well as one of the sliding arms, or pistons, that lift the body to dump its load.

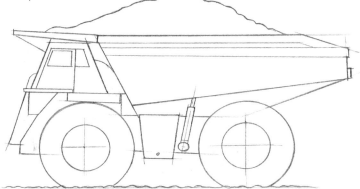

Giant dumper

CRASH, BANG, SCRAPE! Here comes a giant dumper truck full of dirt and rocks from a huge building site or a mine. This truck is more than twice as tall as a grown-up man.

Vrroom!

Finish off by drawing in all the tyre details, filling the body with a mound of rubble, and sketching a stony surface for your dumper to drive on.

Tractor

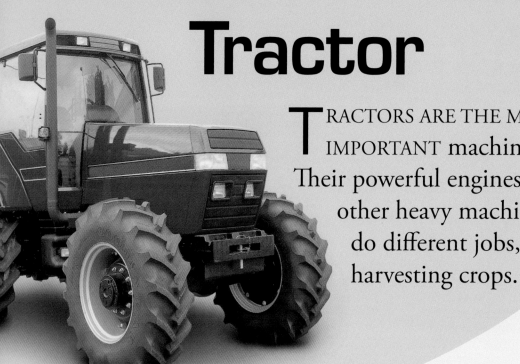

TRACTORS ARE THE MOST IMPORTANT machines on farms. Their powerful engines can pull other heavy machines that do different jobs, like harvesting crops.

1 Use lines for the main body of the tractor, a large circle for the back wheel, and a smaller circle for the front wheel.

2 Give your tractor a door, windows, and a roof. Draw smaller circles inside both wheels.

Rub away any pencil
lines that you don't
need and firm up final
lines with a pen or
dark pencil.

3 Draw even smaller circles inside the wheels. Add some steps, a steering wheel, and a long pipe.

4 Put ridges on the tyres for grip in muddy fields. Add finishing details to the rest of the tractor.

felt tips

A giant dumper's load can weigh as much as 18 elephants. Try to stay out of its way!

Big rollers are meant to flatten new roads, so they are very heavy.

oil pastels

pastels

Look out!

coloured pencils

Big diggers scoop up tonnes (tons) of earth and rock – if you get in the way, they might scoop you up too!

HEAVY MACHINES DO the hard work on farms and building sites. But because they're powerful, they're very dangerous. They're painted in bright colours so people can see them coming.

Tractors have to be very heavy to pull other farm machines.

felt tips

1 Start off by drawing the basic shape of the helicopter. Use curved lines for the top and bottom of the main body and straight lines for the tail.

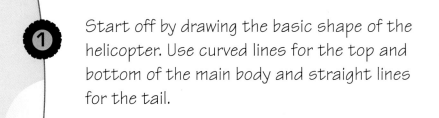

2 Create the shape of the cockpit with two lines at the front of the helicopter. Then add the rotor blades and landing wheels.

3 Add details such as a door and windows. Draw in the smaller rotor blades on the tail of the helicopter.

Whirrrrr

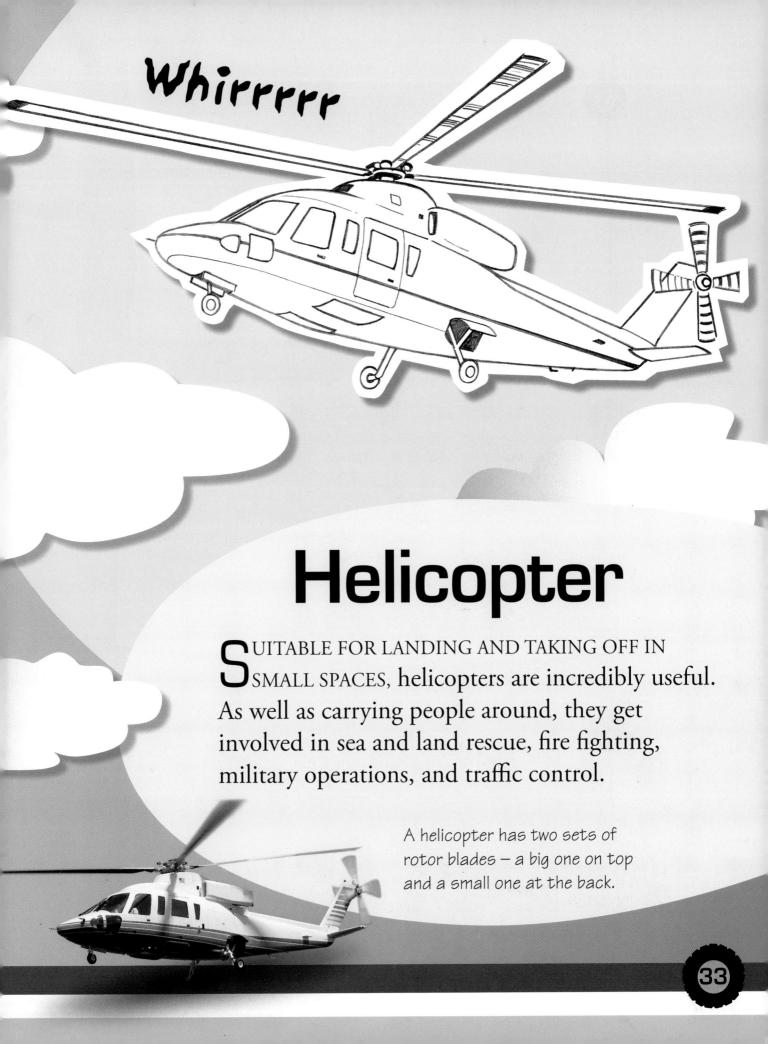

Helicopter

SUITABLE FOR LANDING AND TAKING OFF IN SMALL SPACES, helicopters are incredibly useful. As well as carrying people around, they get involved in sea and land rescue, fire fighting, military operations, and traffic control.

A helicopter has two sets of rotor blades — a big one on top and a small one at the back.

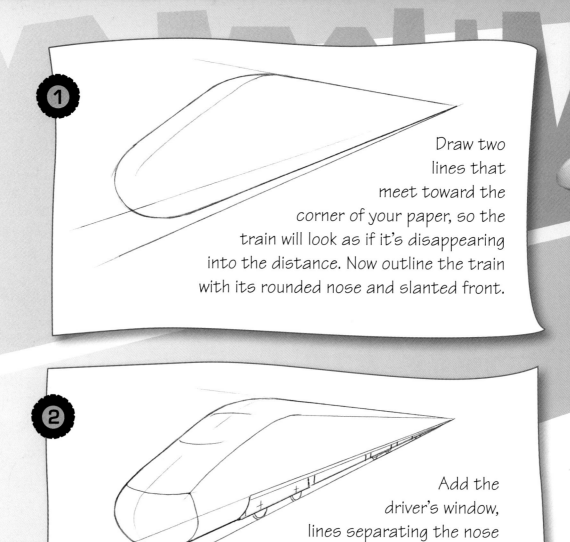

1 Draw two lines that meet toward the corner of your paper, so the train will look as if it's disappearing into the distance. Now outline the train with its rounded nose and slanted front.

2 Add the driver's window, lines separating the nose and the roof from the body, and a few sets of wheels peeking out underneath the carriage.

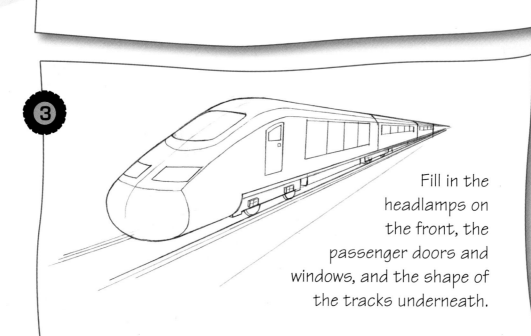

3 Fill in the headlamps on the front, the passenger doors and windows, and the shape of the tracks underneath.

Whoooosh

High-speed train

HERE COMES A HIGH-SPEED train, carrying lots and lots of people very, very fast. These trains run on electricity – some of them get their power from an overhead cable, and some get it from one of their tracks.

Texture

Y OU CAN FIND LOTS OF DIFFERENT TEXTURES on machines. Some machine parts are smooth and shiny (car bonnets and doors) whereas other areas are rough and bumpy (car tyres).

rubber, for smudging

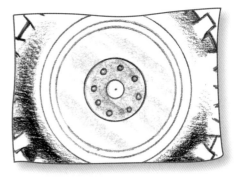

oil pastel, for blending colours

4B soft pencils are thicker than 2B and 3B. Use the right thickness to get the effect you want.

Use a light blue charcoal to make the metal on the tractor wheel look shiny.

2B, 3B, and, 4B soft pencils, for shading

charcoal stick, for blurred edges

soft pastel, also for blending

Vintage car

See how shiny the bonnet and bumper are. Copy the straight lines and shine on the grille.

Words to get you going

bumpy
rubber tracks
shiny **metal**
rough GRITTY
smooth

Tractor
tyres

Get the ridges on your tyres to look 3-D with shading. Charcoal or soft pencils are perfect for making a rough texture.

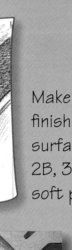

Make an even-looking finish for tyre surfaces using 2B, 3B, and 4B soft pencils.

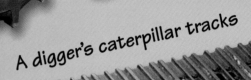
A digger's caterpillar tracks

Car wheel

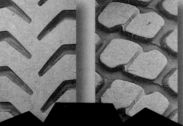
Dumper truck wheels

An HB pencil is good for drawing thin lines and for shading-in areas on the tracks.

Tyres and tracks

Grooves and ridges in tractor tyres and digger caterpillar tracks give the vehicles grip on slippery mud. Recreate the look of grooves and ridges on your drawings.

1 Start off by drawing the bike's basic shape. Remember that the wheels are quite big compared with the body.

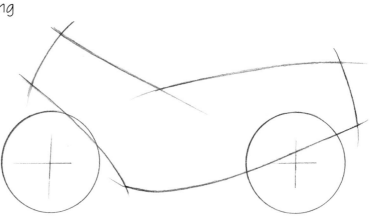

2 Fill in the curvy shapes of the frame, the windscreen, the seat, and the wheel rims. If necessary, pencil in straight lines to guide you, then rub them out later.

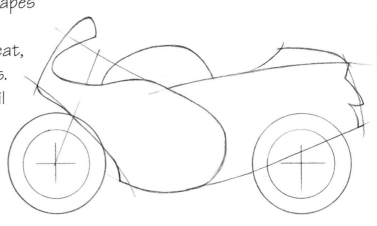

3 Add more details on the body, and important elements such as the handlebars, exhaust, footrest, and the tyre guard.

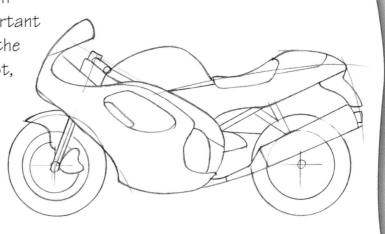

Vroom Vroom

Motorbike

CONTROLLED USING HANDLEBARS instead of a steering wheel, motorbikes have powerful engines, but only two wheels. Sports bikes like this one can reach high speeds very quickly, and turn around sharp corners with no problem at all.

Finish off with realistic touches like air intakes, metalwork, rivets, and subtle shading.

1 Use two long curved lines and one short one to form the speedboat's basic shape. Its frame (called the hull) is pointed at the front so it can cut through water easily.

2 Add squiggly lines to look like the water's surface, and a boxy shape on top of the boat for the windscreen.

3 Add detailing to the hull and windscreen, and a few rippling waves, and sketch the driver in his high-backed seat.

Speedboat

This small, powerful boat bounces through the waves at high speed. It is used in racing, for towing water skiers, as a patrol boat, and just for fun!

Zoooom!

A bit of shading and some extra detailing on the hull will bring your speedboat to life.

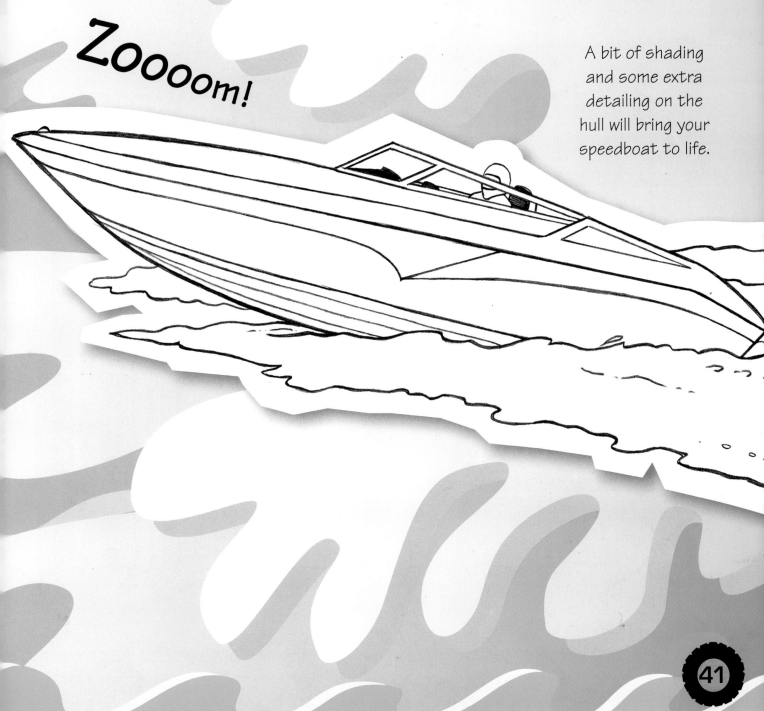

1 Start off with circles and curvy lines for the wheels. Straight lines form the main body of the truck.

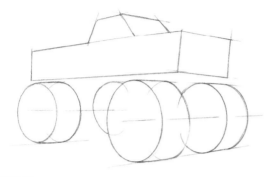

2 Draw smaller circles inside the wheels, curved wheel arches, a light on top of the roof, and a front grille.

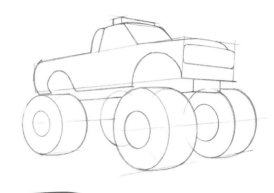

Monster truck

MONSTER TRUCKS are built from pick-up trucks or van bodies. Each one is slightly different. They entertain crowds at large shows by running over cars with their huge wheels and crushing them.

3 Add a wing mirror, a door, suspension bars, headlamps, lines on the front grille, and more detail on the wheels.

4 Give your monster truck some flags and draw the v-shaped tread on the tyres.

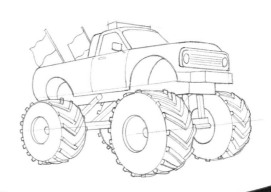

Vrrr-ramm!

Helicopters are used
to fight fires, rescue
people, and take them
to hospital.

pastel

oil pastels

Monster trucks
put on a
fantastic show.

felt tips

High-speed trains whizz people over long distances.

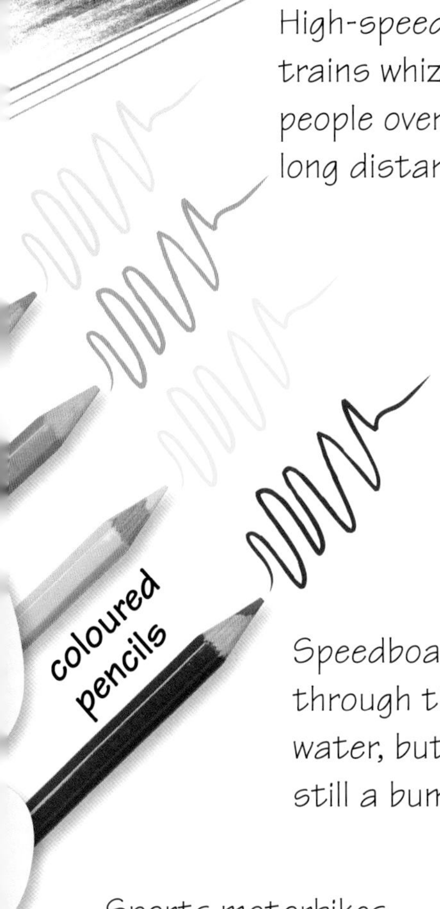

coloured pencils

Watch me!

S OME MACHINES ARE REALLY fun to watch, and their jazzy paintwork makes them even more exciting.

Speedboats cut through the water, but it's still a bumpy ride.

Sports motorbikes make sleek racers.

pastels

oil pastels

Scale

MOST MACHINES ARE TALLER THAN YOU, especially monster trucks! Racing cars are relatively small in scale compared to other vehicles like digger trucks and jumbo jets. If they were too big and bulky they wouldn't win the race!

The largest monster trucks are 4 metres (13.1 feet) tall! Each tyre is 1.68 metres (5.5 feet) high – that's taller than a normal car.

The tailfin on a jumbo jet is 19.42 metres (63.7 feet) high which is as tall as a six-storey building!

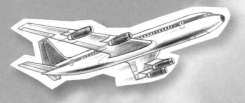

Aeroplanes and helicopters look tiny up in the sky, but when you see them close up they tower above you.

The giant digger needs to be big in order to do its job. It can fill a giant dumper truck in minutes.

Index

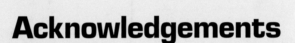

Acknowledgements

Dorling Kindersley would like to thank: Marie Bernadette Greenwood for editorial support; Leah Germann, Tory Gordon-Harris and Jane Bull for design inspiration; Rose Horridge and Claire Bowers for picture research; and Zahavit Shalev for editorial assistance.

Picture credits

Picture credits t = top b = bottom
c= centre l = left r = right

Peter Anderson © Dorling Kindersley 7tr. Brian Cosgrove © Dorling Kindersley (background image 46-47). Andy Crawford © Dorling Kindersley 4tlb, 7tl (Courtesy of Airport); 8tr; 13tc; 18-19; 20-21; 30-31; 36tr; cl, cla, clb; 39tr; 44-45. Mike Dunning © Dorling Kindersley 3br. Mike Dunning © Dorling Kindersley, Courtesy of the National Railway Museum 6c; 35tr. Lynton Gardiner © Dorling Kindersley 14tl. Philip Gatwood © Dorling Kindersley 6bcr. Steve Gorton ©

Dorling Kindersley 7c. Alan Keohane © Dorling Kindersley 13b. © Dorling Kindersley Courtesy of Brookes and Vernons/ JCB. © Dorling Kindersley, Courtesy of Princess Cruises 7cr. © Dorling Kindersley (Courtesy of Goodwood Festival of Speed) 10br; 11bl. Dave King 10cb; 12b; © Dorling Kindersley, Courtesy of the National Motor Museum, Beaulieu 37cl. Richard Leeney © Dorling Kindersley 1cl; 2bl; 5tr; 5crb; 6b; 9tl; 22c; 27tr; 28cr; 37c, tc; 42bl; 47cr; 48br. Eric Meacher © Dorling Kindersley 6bl-7br. NASA 6tl. Ray Moller © Dorling Kindersley, Penton Hook Marine Sales, Surrey 40cl. Gary Ombler © Dorling Kindersley 16tl; 38bl. Tim Ridley © Dorling Kindersley

13cb. Dave Rudkin 11tr; 13tr. Richard Shellabear © Dorling Kindersley, Courtesy of the HET National Automobile Museum, Holland 12cl; 36bl. Chris Stevens 33bl. Matthew Ward © Dorling Kindersley 9tr; 12tr; 13c.